Love & Laughter

Lead to Lasting Happiness

Dr. Ruth Joyce Colbert Barnes

AuthorHouse™
1663 Liberty Drive
Bloomington, IN 47403
www.authorhouse.com
Phone: 1 (800) 839-8640

Published by AuthorHouse 07/16/2018

ISBN: 978-1-5462-5005-0 (sc)
ISBN: 978-1-5462-5006-7 (e)

Library of Congress Control Number: 2018908083

Print information available on the last page.

This book is printed on acid-free paper.

authorHOUSE®

Love & Laughter Lead to Lasting Happiness

Acknowledgements and Appreciation

To my anchor and love of my life, Joseph Barnes (Daddy) Love/Cleve R.J

I have been blessed throughout my life to have great friends...

To: Laurzette Hoggans, my maid of honor, who designed the
cover from one of her beautiful, embroidered quilts

To: Lovely Mia Woodfork, supportive Goddaughter and Foundation partner

To: The fabulous, kind, sweet Kathye Murry, Goddaughter of K Murry

Designs Talent, talent, talent...designs, edits, transcribes

Special thanks to...

Sharon Dean of Dean's Typesetting for her support
Paula McDade of Stellar Media who provided photography for this book
Ayanna Najuma of Lincoln McLeod- Journalist & Media

Introduction

This book is intended to contain both an inspirational and Health & Wellness message. We have within us the ability to create, promote, and maintain good mental health. Our attitudes about caring for our bodies, adhering to good principles of healthy nutrition and the prevention of illness and disease. If we want to maintain healthful living, it requires physical, mental, and spiritual knowledge to avoid disease and maintain the type of life filled with laughter, joy, happiness, health, and healing. In order to be healed if illness occurs our mind, body, and spirit must be harmoniously in sync if recovery and restoration is favorable. A life full of mental peace, joy, love, and caring for others benefits the caring person and the person who is being cared for.

This book offers us a grand reminder that love is a powerful healer and that laughter and humor, along with good nutrition, when eaten and assimilated into our bodies gives us great strength to the mind and body. This book has given us the insight that if you can laugh and love someone that God will provide a happier life for you.

Knowledge is power and we have a great opportunity to maintain health and restore it to some degree if illness occurs, we can assist our health professionals by creating a reform in the way we eat and think influencing and controlling our mental processes. Lifestyle changes are an initial powerful step toward long lasting anti-aging and true happiness.

Table of Contents

Chapter

1

Dr. Ruth Joyce Colbert Barnes and her husband Joseph Barnes, pictured here
at the beginning of their marriage, have been married for 45 years.

"Real love requires a commitment and a true sense if caring to be effective and believable."

Chapter One

The Healing Power of Love

Love has a tremendous impact on your health, healing, and emotional well-being. There are many studies dealing with the power of some form of love expression upon healing and stress reduction, from the simple love of a pet to the love shown by families. These experiences showed a significant decrease in blood pressure, respiration rates, heart rates, and all aspects of the factors relating to stress increase.

Love should be celebrated daily by just saying, "I love you" to someone. Say it with meaning, say it with conviction - just say it.

Love comes in many forms. You must make room in your life for love. Make room in your heart to receive love. Holding on to the past can sometimes prove to block true love and positive feelings. Each person really deserves love and respect. However, you will find that you must offer love to receive it.

Real love requires a commitment and a true sense of caring to be effective and believable. Love is a great investment. Friendship and relationships must be formed and cultivated.

We must keep believing in the power of love in our relationships. Our relationships with others mean everything. The way we react and communicate with others is gravel y important. Take the time to really look at your life as it relates to those around you. An empowered person can impact everyone they encounter. Showing love can help you conquer & endure anything. Love breeds hope and happiness; it breeds encouragement; it helps everything become an opportunity for growth, expansion, respect, and harmony.

Over the next few months and years, my goal is to empower people with the understanding that some of the most beautiful things in the world come from within. As Helen Keller said, "They cannot be seen or touched; they must be felt with the heart." We will naturally find great love with our families, however I want to explore the divine pleasure in true friendships. A good friend will often times bring such pleasure and joy to your life; it will inspire you and make your day-to-day life so full of creativity and happiness that it makes your life seem like sheer fun to be alive.

As I mentioned earlier, the special people in your life are the real basis for the power and purpose of your daily happiness. If you make good choices and work at fostering good relationships, it fuels your very soul. This approach to defer stresses helps to motivate you, comfort you, and make you an unstoppable force. Make dedicated time for you and your friends or loved ones.

Chapter 2

"*There is only one of you, so be unique.*"

Chapter Two

Positive Self-Regard (Self-Esteem & Self Love)

Positive self-regard allows you to enjoy yourself and be happy with who you are. This regard for yourself does not mean that you stop striving to be the best you can be.

There is only one of you, so *be unique*. Celebrate your own successes and realize and change your losses. When issues and challenges come along, go for them with gusto - *Beat the Odds*:

- Rather than being your own worst enemy, analyze the situation closely and look for several types of resources to arrive at a solution to conquer the issue.

- Find ways to deflate issues before they get out of hand and all blown up. Start early with small power breaks; challenges revitalize you and help you think clearer and wiser.

- Learn to deliver self-praise and mental applause.

- Daily activities can sometimes bring a mixture of discouragement and hassles. This mixture must be countered immediately with some type of encouraging act.

- Break your known bad habits. Very often when things happen we blame ourselves and adopt habits that make matters worse. Find the coping mechanisms that really work for you.

- Build new and better solutions. Control your situation. Identify weak areas and strive to strengthen them.

- Develop new strategies for problem solving. Remember to be your own cheerleader.

- Handle each problem with confidence. In order to maintain a positive self-regard stance, you must understand and realize that your mind is powerful and strongly controls how you feel about yourself. It becomes very easy to have and feel anxiety, anger, and depression.

With the day-to-day hassles, we can easily exhibit resentment, worry, and humiliation. Observe what's happening when you feel these discomforts. Keep a journal and notice the trouble spots; conquer them early with simple, positive reactions. Amazingly, the hassles become less and less troublesome because your confidence builds and you begin to handle them so much better.

In order to maintain your positive self-regard, you must keep your mind and spirit on the positive side by avoiding negative situations, negative conservations, and negative people.

Be at home with your self-image. If you are not happy with yourself, develop a plan to change those things you are unhappy with. Develop a realistic set of goals for improvement. Target any trouble spots that you know will take time in the improvement process.

The great solutions in life (for your life) come from you and the choices you make. In every way, try to *do what you love* and what you do with it is up to you. Even if you must spend your day helping someone unexpectedly, that's okay. The love and spirit in which you do it means everything, to you and the recipient of your assistance. It is a win, win situation for all.

Chapter

3

> *"One of the major obstacles in life is that we become unhappy with what we have."*

Chapter Three

One Cup of Tea, One Day at a Time: A Formula for Happiness and Love

The question is, "How do I get to the good place in my life?" This is the question that many of us ask ourselves regarding love, laughter, and happiness. In today's society we are all full of anxiety, frustration, and stress. Most of us are living our lives in overdrive.

If you are overwhelmed by the demands and daily stresses of life, you need the following to happen while getting to your good place of happiness:

- Stop and smell the roses; take one cup of tea, one day at a time.
- Identify the mental state that's driving your anxiety or frustration.

Often you can't make the connection until you stop and revisit what is driving your frustration.

- Acknowledge the difficulties. Remove any road blocks or at least minimize them; they can often be eliminated.
- Let go of fears (we all have them). Many times we fail to identify them as fears that are unfounded.
- Pinpoint the frustration triggers.
- Write down everything that is nagging or bugging you. Try again and again to gain insight into what is causing them, and most importantly identify where they are coming from.

There are many times in life when we must *spring clean* our lives, clean out the cob webs, throw out the old and bring in the new - new thoughts and attitudes.

One of the major obstacles in life is that we become unhappy with what we have. We need to cut out the extra stress and worry and learn to be happier with what we have. We must not kid ourselves, most happiness takes work to happen.

It is amazing that happiness very often comes from places and things of surprise. Embrace the power of surprise in your loving actions toward others in your daily encounters and activities. Simple little surprise moments bring unexpected happiness. It is up to you to bring energy into your life which translates into a light, playful vibe, lifting the spirits of everyone in the room with you.

When you take time to stop and smell the roses, you realize all of the things that you are at peace with and think about all of the things that you are grateful for. You can experience great joy in thinking about them. The frustration that drives you may seem too much to take at times and can be triggered by one's own imagination or state of mind and environment. Streamline your activities, be checked by your health professional, and make sure your health is in a good state. We all need to first evaluate what we need to do to enlighten ourselves and find out about each aspect of our own health in order to maintain. If all is well, great, but also check your environment.

Chapter
4

"*The key to happiness is the ability to create moments of fun and laughter within your life.*"

Chapter Four

Good Mental Health is the Key to Laughter & Happiness

We must all develop a mindset for happiness. Identify those things in your life that create unhappiness and work toward changing them. Now, we all know that change is easy to talk about and discuss but actually making it happen is another story. Here are some simple, easy steps toward small changes and actions toward creating a happier life:

1. Start by spring cleaning your life; clear out those things which clutter your thoughts.
2. Health is a great part of being happy. You must commit to keeping yourself in the best of shape both physically and mentally.
3. The key to happiness is the ability to create moments of fun and laughter within your life. Have moments when you want to eat cheese fries or a real burger without allowing the wrath of guilt to take over your life. Please, however, stick to your healthy eating habits at least 95 percent of the time.

Remember, we can help to heal our lives. We can create great thoughts by doing positive affirmations and planting positive seeds daily in our lives and others. Most individuals possess an internal self-love list, we just have to reach inside and pull it out. We must not be afraid to think positive things about ourselves. If we think we are these things, then just imagine we will become those positive things. Let us prepare ourselves. What is your list? Start today.

I believe...

    1.) I am a loving person.
    2.) I have a sense of humor (certainly regarding myself).
    3.) I am a caring person.
    4.) I am health conscious.
    5.) I am basically smart.
    6.) I have a giving spirit.
    7.) I have an open mind.
    8.) I am successful.

Come on now, make your list. Stick to it, say it, mean it, do it, and live it!

Each person should have an awareness of what mental or physical activities help them to build self-confidence. We must build up our inward talent in everything we do, thereby building our own success tool chest.

Positive attitudes help us to conquer burdens and conflict. Undue sadness produces a risk to our health and mindset that is often hard to overcome. It is clear to me that if we look for the simplest and smallest kindness from people that surprisingly it goes a long way to help us fight depression or loneliness, it even inspires us to carry on and be grateful. The kind deeds of others can be so valuable to us; they are hidden bits of beauty in our everyday life that we just need to be very thankful for.

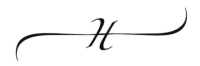

Chapter
5

"*One of the best anti-aging antidotes is to love every day,*
every hour, every minute that you have been given."

Chapter Five

Laughter is the Anti-Aging Antidote for Happiness

In order to be happy for a lifetime, grow flowers, contemplate the vibrant hues, delicate shades, and wide variety of colors which all hold one of the keys to happiness, and happiness holds the power of life. Learn to immerse yourself in the wonder of our beautiful environment. Meditate daily to relieve the stresses of the day. It allows you to age in peaceful tranquility.

There is beauty and splendor in the breathtaking foliage around us, the trees, flowers, shrubs, and stunning landscapes. Every town has these wonderful spots, so find one and become inspired with its beauty.

Celebrate your life every day. One of the best anti-aging antidotes is to love every day, every hour, every minute that you have been given. It shows on your face. It shows with your body language. People will be able to pick up your vibe, pick up your inspiration, and see your vibrant, alive look.

One of life's riches is to truly understand that each day in your life is a blessing. We should give thanks for the gift of another day to do something wonderful.

The antidote of a smile (not a fake one), but a truly happy expression does wonders for your body chemistry. It is contagious, just try it.

When we sleep well, we age better. Our environment can work against a good night's sleep, therefore sometimes, we need to assess our bedroom for sleep distractors. Minor changes can correct this immediately; take away electronic distractors from your bed chamber. Make your bedroom as clutter free as possible. Keep the area cool, cut your light down, cover up your clock, check out any noise distractors and eliminate them. This is a really good start at adjusting your lifestyle and assisting in simple anti-aging approaches.

The morning can be our mental haze producer, if you feel foggy or groggy, that can be very normal. Sometimes if you don't give your body and brain a jumpstart, even after a good night's sleep, this may last 2 to 3 hours. The first thing you need is the bright light of day. Switch on your light and rev your memory and reaction time with food. Get out the oatmeal; experts say that it provides a good, balanced supply of glucose that fuels the brain and assists in improving the memory.

Good nutrition and water are great antidotes for the aging process. Be forever young.

Chapter

6

"*Joy and laughter in someone's life is a powerful healer.*"

Chapter Six

Find Humor in All That You Do

Humor requires that you demonstrate passion -- a stunning passion for the unusual, for the plain & simple act of fun. Immerse yourself in things that bring laughter into your life. If you are to be happy for a lifetime and not just for a fleeting moment, you must not take everything so seriously and especially yourself. One of the greatest things to remember is that many of the grandest delights and times you may encounter comes from the tiniest acts of love and thoughtfulness.

There are countless possibilities for laughter if you look for ways to make someone else happy and celebrate your special findings together.

Joy and laughter in someone's life is a powerful healer. Having worked with cancer patients during their treatment stage, it should be noted that finding something they can smile about helps then better cope with their treatment.

Laughter makes your feel good inside. Please locate all of the places and identify all of the things that make you happy and try to recreate them. If it is good food, have French Day, Italian day of a slamming soul food day. All dishes can be made in a healthy manner.

Life can be full of fun and riches if you take the time. Only you can determine how to use it. If you use your time wisely and carefully, life becomes easier, less stressful and less complex.

Begin expressing yourself with joy. Create, collect and celebrate. If you can't take a vacation, find all of the many wonderful fun-filled, inexpensive things to enjoy right under your nose. Plan a great salad lunch at your premier shopping center. Get out and go!

Find your fine arts district; most cities have them. It is a great getaway. Just coast up and down the various shops. Great deals can be found for just pennies! Find outdoor adventures for your family. Cities now have concerts, live music, and fun for everyone to enjoy at no or very low cost.

The simple things can make us happy; we just have to realize the rewards. Small gestures are powerful. The power and reward of being respectful and polite to someone and their kind, gracious response can bring us simple joy.

Chapter

7

"*Learn to appreciate aging, for there are many wonderful things that occur with getting older.*"

Chapter Seven

Old Women/Old Men- Aging Means Happiness

We should learn to love, embrace, and be grateful for aging, be beautiful, bold, and not just old at any age. Look for all of the positives for aging gaining confidence, knowing that you are better than ever, acknowledging wisdom and becoming comfortable with yourself. Mental reversal of the words old man, old woman. Learn to appreciate aging, for there are many wonderful things that occur with getting older.

Everyone has essentials in their lives. Anti-aging requires rejuvenation, redefining, and re-strategizing your essentials in life.

Take time to discover your essentials:

- There are moments of promise in your life. I refer to these moments as life's balance moments.
- We all need to cultivate and radiate thoughtful reflections because they inspire faith.
- One of our real-life essentials is surviving and thriving.

Anti-aging is really healthy beauty. It's all about increasing the production of collagen that your body naturally produces. The gentle cleansing process of all areas of the body is most important. Old men/old women is just a tongue & cheek statement and is merely fun for us; we believe there really is no old anywhere, just seasoned. Healthy beauty starts with good, healthy foods, ample water, and lots of veggies and fruits. Rejuvenate and transfom1 your skin with good, healthy lifestyle activities (e.g. sleeping well, hydration, and good teeth repair. Try eating special skin-friendly vitamin A and C foods such as kale, broccoli, cauliflower, and brussel sprouts. Salmon provides you with Omega-3 fats. Some studies have shown that fish, especially those having Omega-3, may help keep cancer cells from spreading or growing. You should have two to three servings per week, also sardines and mackerel are good fish solutions.

Heal thy hair becomes gorgeous when cleansing with non-harsh products, conditioning, and nourishing. This is an inside and outside method to beauty and anti-aging. We all want radiant, supple, smooth skin. Dr. Debra Juliman, M.D., author of Skin Rules says, "We need low-glycemic foods. High-glycemic foods are known to cause acne and wrinkles." Feel good and be happy about longevity. It is totally possible to like seasoning.

Chapter

8

"Stay motivated and remember to find laughter."

Chapter Eight

Laughter: A Relief from Depression

Depression can be very devastating to you and your family members.

Good mental and social interactions are paramount and stimulating to your mental health. Daily exercise and being active can stimulate hormones that produce a feeling of well-being

Laughter has always been the best medicine to lift your spirits and release some of the walls of depression. The health professionals are very necessary during depression and your medical routine is important. Many solutions are centered around you knowing that you are taking a central role in your own healthcare which can help keep anxiety and your emotions from getting out of control.

There are several methods to relieve anxiety and stress: ten to thirty minutes of meditation each day helps you to center and ground yourself and get your emotions in check, breathe, inhale deeply, exhale slowly, slow your breathing patterns and breathing rate. This approach automatically stimulates your normal body relaxation response. Depression can be overcome, so your part and stay compliant with any medication you have been prescribed. Get restful sleep and eat a healthy diet. Become a champion of your own health and well-being every day. Find the humor in life, it's there, simple, fresh, and great medicine in laughter.

1. Relief from Depression (Self-help ideas to follow)
2. Relief Reasoning
   a. Share your feelings. It is liberating to share the hurt or problem; this helps you face your feelings and not keep them buried inside.
   b. Don 't take every negative incident personally. Sometimes it isn't just you. It can be the other person or the situation. The challenge is to be able to surge past the negative and not just thrive or dote on it. Immediately find a positive person or situation to connect with. Stay motivated and remember to find laughter.
   c. Visualize success, and smile about each small victory.
   d. Be thankful.

Chapter

9

"*Good, healthy habits work beautifully to empower you and slow down the aging proce*"

Chapter Nine

Empowerment Begins with Knowledge

Life has great rhythm. We must empower ourselves with knowledge so that we can just dive into it. The more we learn, the more remarkable and incredible we can become. It all begins with self-understanding and self-expression. We are often placed in cycles that are started by us or others. Cycles of lack of expectation, cycles of disappointment, and cycles of depression.

Self-examination is essential to breaking these critical cycles with in our life systems. There are many imperfect moments which can occur and may trigger any of these critical cycles. The more comfortable we become with ourselves, the more we can accept and start to improve those personal areas that need work and forward movement.

Empowerment begins with positive self-expression which begins with confidence-building actions. We will become very aware of our strengths, build upon them and conquer our weaknesses.

A very good place to start with is to take control of your lifestyle. Good, healthy habits work beautifully to empower you and slow down the aging process. Good nutrition (which includes a diet rich in antitoxins with colorful fruits and vegetables) and fitness.

In every aspect of your well-being, you must learn about taking care of yourself. Knowledge is Health Power! It does not matter what age you are, you need to learn about the status of your own health and start to maintain healthy habits. We must make being uninformed or unknowledgeable a thing of the past. Discover what a lift it gives you to learn what it takes to care for yourself. There are many significant medical advances that assist us in longevity.

Chapter

10

"How can you be depressed in hot pink
lace (and only you know it)?"

Chapter Ten

Cute Lingerie in Great Colors Lifts the Spirit

The dress in your closet and the pants hanging over the door must belong to someone else because they just don't fit! Who shrunk your jeans on purpose? Who smashed your self-image? The mid-section on both you and hubby have gone south. Are we both in menopause?

Let's start looking better because it makes you feel better. You hear this all the time, let's do it. Do an analysis on what makes you look better or feel better - a good workout, a pedicure, massage, facial.

Wear something every day that you really love, it may be just a scarf or shoes...a flashy belt. Make it a point to use your favorite colors; it lifts your spirit if you have the courage. Realize that you Jet the walls down in your life and live the best life that you can.

Cute lingerie in great colors that you love can lift your spirits. The real prescription for a lifetime of wellness is to reduce stressors in your life. Most of us are just juggling too much. It can produce very risky health consequences such as heart disease, depression, obesity, and many other conditions.

Get more sleep, Jack of it can cause inability to concentrate and make sound decisions. Proactively manage your happiness, improve your attitude, enjoy yourself, and do something your yourself every day.

What occasion are you saving the good stuff for? Beautiful, cute opps! Lingerie with shameless, in-your-face colors, and lots of perky I am fun attitude is just the thing to upgrade your mood. They should be only for you. How can you be depressed in hot pink lace (and only you know it)? What a great secret for smiles to keep you smiling and no one knows why.

Chapter

11

"You have the power to make happiness a life-long habit."

Chapter Eleven

Long Lasting Happiness (It's a Habit)

The American author, E. Hubbard says, "Happiness is a habit – cultivate it."

When circumstances come our way, very often we are not the cause. No matter how hard we try, we have no control or very little control. These instances tend to anger us, make us depressed, or sadden our days. The thing that we must realize is that we have choices and can change how we react to difficult things that happen to us. Sometimes our reaction is appropriate; however, the real choice is not to be negative.

If we look at life on the positive side, it helps us have better coping skills when depression or negative things occur. Try to seek out friends and individuals who have captured the power of happiness and joy as a way of life. They tend to have a brighter outlook and happiness as a means of combating negative conditions and adversity.

Remember...

- You have the ability to choose how you react to a situation.
- You choose (not events) what makes you happy or unhappy.
- You have the power to make happiness a life-long habit.
- Exhibit gratitude and appreciation.
- Spirituality, prayer, and meditation all give your life meaning.

Make a bold move toward controlling your future. Be courageous, sure, and confident about your health. It is incredible what this move will do for your life and happiness. You need to appreciate your circle of support, friends, family, colleagues, and loved ones.

We all have personal challenges, but we must become focused and dedicated to understanding that Health is very important to happiness. Lifestyle modifications and a plan plays a key part in living a longer, healthier life. Join me, Blessings & Peace.

About the Author

Dr. Ruth Joyce Colbert Barnes is the principal of R.J. Colbert Enterprises, Inc., international consultants and developers. She is also CEO of the Dr. Ruth Joyce Colbert Barnes Foundation, Inc. and the Colbert Institute of Health and Wellness. Dr. Barnes has many years of experience as an inspirational/motivational speaker and consultant. To obtain information about her services as a speaker or consultant or to purchase books and CDs, please visit her at www.rjcbfoundation.org. Please also like us on Facebook. Thank you!

Contact information:

Dr. Ruth Joyce Colbert Barnes
Post Office Box 14615
Oklahoma City, Oklahoma 73113
E-mail: rjcb@rjcbfoundation.org
Website: www.rjcbfoundation.org
Facebook: www.facebook.com/rjcbosafcollaborationgfoundations

Printed in the United States
By Bookmasters